Fun Holiday Crafts Kids Can Do!

Kwanzaa Crafts

Carol Gnojewski

E **Enslow Publishers, Inc.**

40 Industrial Road   PO Box 38
Box 398   Aldershot
Berkeley Heights, NJ 07922   Hants GU12 6BP
USA   UK

http://www.enslow.com

Many thanks to Tasleem Qaasim and Yvonne Terrell-Powell
of Shoreline Community College, Shoreline, WA,
for their inspiration and insight.

Library of Congress Cataloging-in-Publication Data

Gnojewski, Carol.
    Kwanzaa crafts / Carol Gnojewski.
        p. cm. — (Fun holiday crafts kids can do)
    Summary: Provides information about the origin and customs of Kwanzaa, ideas for celebrating
this holiday, and directions for making such crafts as people dolls, a centerpiece, and African clothes.
    ISBN 0-7660-2203-X (hardcover)
    1. Kwanzaa decorations—Juvenile literature. 2. Handicraft—Juvenile literature. [1. Kwanzaa
decorations. 2. Handicraft.] I. Title. II. Series.
TT900.K92G56 2004
745.594'1612—dc22
                                                                2003012075

Printed in the United States of America

10 9 8 7 6 5 4 3 2 1

To Our Readers:
We have done our best to make sure all Internet Addresses in this book were active and appropriate
when we went to press. However, the author and the publisher have no control over and assume
no liability for the material available on those Internet sites or on other Web sites they may link to.
Any comments or suggestions can be sent by e-mail to comments@enslow.com or to the address
on the back cover.

Illustration Credits: Crafts prepared by June Ponte. Photography by Carl Feryok.

Cover Photos: Carl Feryok

Contents

*Safety Note: Be sure to ask for help from an adult, if needed, to complete these crafts!

introduction

Kwanzaa is a family holiday that lasts from December 26 to January 1. Dr. Maulana Karenga, a professor, and his friends created Kwanzaa in 1966. They wanted African Americans to have a special holiday to celebrate family and community.

They also wanted people to learn about Africa. During Kwanzaa, families place special African symbols in their homes. The symbols and activities of Kwanzaa have Swahili names. Swahili is an African language. *Kwanzaa* comes from a phrase that means "first fruits" in Swahili.

In Swahili, the seven days of Kwanzaa are:

Day 1:
Umoja
(oo-MOE-jah)
unity

Day 5:
Nia
(nee-AH)
purpose

Day 2:
Kujichagulia
(koo-jee-cha-goo-LEE-ah)
self-determination

Day 6:
Kuumba
(koo-OOM-bah)
creativity

Day 3:
Ujima
(oo-JEE-mah)
group work

Day 7:
Imani
(ee-MAH-nee)
faith

Day 4:
Ujamaa
(oo-JAH-mah)
cooperative economics

These ideas are called *nguzo saba* (en-GOO-zoh sah-BAH), or the seven principles. Think about these seven ideas of Kwanzaa as you make the crafts in this book and enjoy the week-long holiday.

Seven Candles Game

The Swahili name for this game is mishumaa saba (mee-SHOO-mah SAH-bah). Each day during Kwanzaa, a candle is lit in the kinara (kee-NAH-rah), or candleholder.

The center candle is black for the African people. It is lit on the first day of Kwanzaa. The other six candles are red and green. Red means blood and standing up for your beliefs. Green stands for hopes and dreams.

What You Will Need:

- red, green, and black permanent markers
- poster paint (optional)
- paintbrush (optional)
- newspaper
- drinking straws
- scissors

1. Cut each straw into thirds. You will need twenty-one straw pieces.

2. Spread out some newspaper to keep your workspace clean. Use the markers or poster paint to color the straw pieces to look like Kwanzaa candles. Make three straws black, nine straws red, and nine straws green.

3. Let the straws dry.

4. Play following the rules of Pick-Up Sticks. Hold the "candles" in one hand so they are facing up and down. Put the bottoms of the candles on the floor or a table. Let go quickly. The candles will scatter as they fall.

5. Pick up one candle at a time. If any other candles move, your turn is over. The first player to pick up the seven candles of the *kinara* (one black, three red, three green) wins.

Start with a handful of straws...

Cut and then color them with the markers...

Enjoy the game with your family and friends!

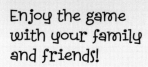

Holiday Hint:

Another way to play is to continue the game until all the candles have been picked up. The winner is the player with the most points. Black candles are fifteen points. Red candles are ten points. Green candles are five points.

People Dolls

African dolls are often given to children as zawadi (sah-WAH-dee), or gifts, during Kwanzaa. But not all people who celebrate Kwanzaa are Africans or African Americans. People all over the world honor this holiday.

What You Will Need:

- crayons or markers
- poster paint (optional)
- paintbrush (optional)
- pipe cleaners
- wooden doll pins or clothespins
- white glue
- colored yarn or embroidery thread
- scissors

1. Use crayons, markers, or poster paint to color the "head" of the doll pins or clothespins.

2. Spread glue down the length of the pin.

3. Start at the bottom and wrap yarn or thread around the legs. Do not overlap the yarn or thread. Press the yarn or thread into the glue. To make pants, wrap each leg separately. For a dress, wrap the yarn or thread around both legs. Glue the end of the yarn or thread to the doll pin or clothespin about halfway up.

4. Use a different color yarn or thread to wrap the top half of the doll. Cut the yarn or thread and glue the end to the doll pin. Draw a face with the crayons or markers.

5. Glue on extra yarn or thread pieces for hair.

6. Glue a pipe cleaner to the doll's back. Bend it to make arms.

Color the "head" of
the clothespin. . .

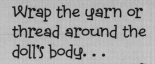

Wrap the yarn or
thread around the
doll's body. . .

Use crayons, markers,
and pipe cleaners to add
the finishing touches to
your doll!

Holiday Hint:

These dolls make wonderful
gifts to exchange during
Kwanzaa. Arrange them on a
mkeka (m-KAY-cah), or mat. Or,
string several dolls together as a
family garland.

9

Two-Sides-of-Me Flip Mask

Africans wear masks during tribal dances and other celebrations. A mask can hide your face or show others who you are inside.

What You Will Need:

- scissors
- construction paper
- white glue
- paper plate or cardboard circle
- magazines (optional)
- crayons or markers
- large craft sticks or tongue depressors
- feathers, fabric, stickers, or other craft items

1. Cut two large triangles from construction paper to fit inside the paper plate or cardboard circle.

2. Glue a triangle on one side of the plate.

3. Glue the second triangle on the other side of the plate.

4. Look through magazines for facial features, or simply draw your own. Glue eyes on both triangles or cut out eyeholes. Glue a mouth and a nose on each triangle.

5. Decorate the two sides of your mask with crayons or markers. Glue on feathers, fabric, stickers, or other craft items.

6. Glue the craft sticks to either side of the mask where your ears would be. Now you can flip the mask to reveal two sides of you!

Start by gluing triangles to each side of the plate...

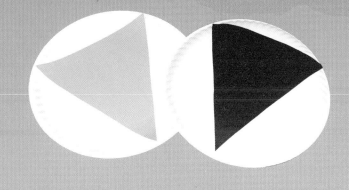

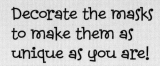

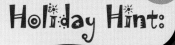

Add the eyes, nose, and mouth...

Decorate the masks to make them as unique as you are!

Holiday Hint:

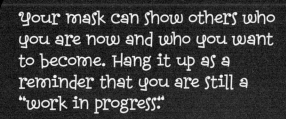

Your mask can show others who you are now and who you want to become. Hang it up as a reminder that you are still a "work in progress."

Storytelling Stick

In western Africa, griots (GREE-ohs) were the storytellers. Songs, wise sayings, and histories were not written down. Griots learned them and shared them aloud.

In the Akan tribes of Ghana in western Africa, people called okyeames (oh-kay-YAH-mays) are like griots. They carry special sticks, or staffs, called pomas (POH-mahs). The carvings on top of their staffs tell a message.

What You Will Need:

- newspaper
- tape
- aluminum foil
- crepe paper
- yarn, string, or colored pipe cleaners (optional)
- feathers (optional)
- black, red, and green tissue paper (optional)

1. Place three or four sheets of newspaper on top of one another.

2. Pick up one corner and roll the newspaper toward the opposite corner.

3. Tape the rolled paper closed.

4. Wrap a sheet of aluminum foil around the top end of the newspaper stick. Shape the foil into a ball, hook, or animal to make a handle.

5. Tape strips of crepe paper to the stick for color. Or, tie yarn around the foil top. If you like, add feathers between the yarn and the newspaper.

Start by rolling the newspaper. . .

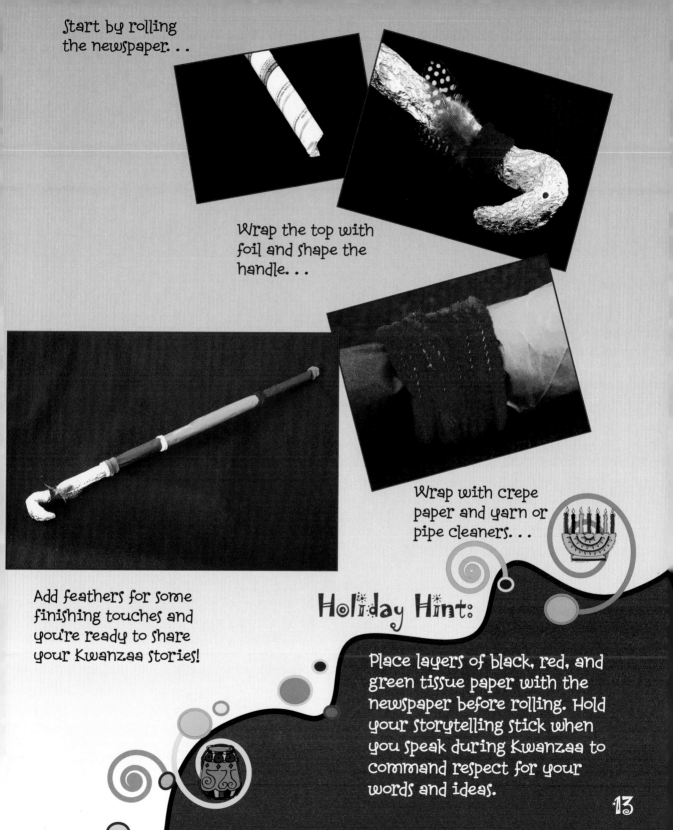

Wrap the top with foil and shape the handle. . .

Wrap with crepe paper and yarn or pipe cleaners. . .

Add feathers for some finishing touches and you're ready to share your Kwanzaa stories!

Holiday Hint:

Place layers of black, red, and green tissue paper with the newspaper before rolling. Hold your storytelling stick when you speak during Kwanzaa to command respect for your words and ideas.

13

Rolled Paper Beads

In African countries, beads decorate everything from clothes and headbands to baskets and drums. Some people use beads as money. Beads can also tell others what job a person has in the community.

What You Will Need:

- scissors
- colored paper
- white glue
- pencil
- baking sheet or other flat, nonstick surface
- glitter (optional)
- elastic thread

1. Use scissors to cut long, thin triangles from colored paper.

2. Spread glue over the top of a triangle. Cover it completely.

3. Place the pencil on the widest end of the triangle and roll the paper and pencil together toward the point of the triangle. Carefully, slide the pencil out of the rolled paper bead.

4. Place the beads on a baking tray or other flat, nonstick surface to dry.

5. To make the beads stronger, cover the outside of them with glue. Sprinkle them with glitter to add sparkle. Let the beads dry.

6. Trim the ends of the dried beads with scissors.

7. String the beads on elastic thread to make necklaces, bracelets, anklets, and armbands.

Start with some colored paper. . .

Roll into colorful beads and add glitter. . .

String them together. . .

Your beads are now ready for you to wear or give as gifts!

Holiday Hint:

Make rolled paper beads to decorate Kwanzaa projects. Or, use the paper beads for gifts or trade with friends.

Home Bank

Ujamaa is a day to share your money and your skills. Make a home bank to save coins during the year.

What You Will Need:

- small milk or whipping cream carton
- tape or stapler
- pencil
- construction paper
- scissors
- white glue
- markers
- small items (beans, lentils, yarn, sticks, etc.)

1. Wash and dry an empty milk or cream carton well.

2. Close the carton opening with tape or staple it shut.

3. Trace the sides of the carton onto construction paper.

4. Cut out the paper pieces. Glue them to the outside of the carton.

5. Use markers to decorate your home bank. Add craft items, such as beans for doorknobs, yarn or pipe cleaners for doors and windows, and small craft sticks for shutters.

6. Have an adult cut a slit on the top of the bank large enough to drop in coins.

Start with a milk carton...

Trace the sides and cut the construction paper...

Decorate the carton with small craft items. You now have a great bank!

Holiday Hint:

Ask family members to help you save money. When the bank is full, open it up. As a family, decide how best to spend the money.

Basket Centerpiece

In Africa, cloth and baskets are woven from natural materials, such as wool and grass. The Zulu tribes of South Africa weave the bottom of a basket first. They call the bottom part "the mother." The rest of the basket is "the baby" that grows strand by strand.

What You Will Need:

- heavy string or yarn
- plastic berry basket
- scissors
- twist ties
- rolled beads (optional—see page 14)
- napkin
- fruits and vegetables

1. Tie the string or yarn to one corner of the basket near the bottom.

2. Working upward, wrap the string or yarn around the basket.

3. Keep wrapping until you reach the top of the basket. Cut the string or yarn and tie the end to the basket rim.

4. Poke twist ties through the basket holes. Twist the ties twice. Add ties in different places around the basket to keep the string or yarn in place.

5. Put rolled beads (see page 14) on the twist tie ends and bend them toward the bead.

6. Place a napkin inside the basket.

7. Fill the basket with small *mazao* (mah-ZAH-oh)—fruits and vegetables, such as cherry tomatoes, baby carrots, or dates.

Start by wrapping your basket with string or yarn...

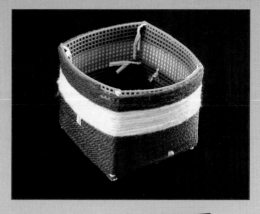

Add some decorative beads...

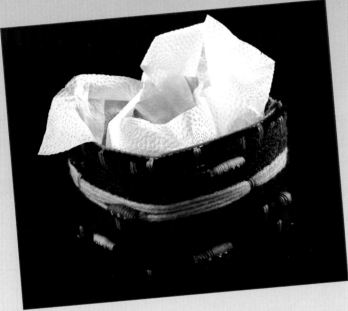

Place a napkin inside and fill your completed basket with symbols of Kwanzaa!

Holiday Hint:

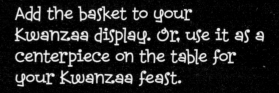

Add the basket to your Kwanzaa display. Or, use it as a centerpiece on the table for your Kwanzaa feast.

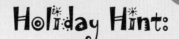

African Clothes

African clothes are often made from dyed and woven cotton or wool. The fabric is worn loosely draped around the body. African women cover their hair with a gele (GAY-lay), or head wrap. Men wear long pieces of cloth around their shoulders.

What You Will Need:

- tape measure or ruler
- pencil
- old sheet or light-colored cotton fabric (ask for permission!)
- scissors
- markers
- fabric paints and paintbrush (optional)
- rolled paper beads (optional)

1. Use a tape measure or ruler to mark a rectangle 9 by 45 inches on an old sheet or light-colored fabric. Cut out the rectangle.

2. Draw patterns on the material using markers. If you like, use the patterns on pages 27–29.

3. Color your patterns with fabric paint. If you do not have fabric paint, markers will work just as well.

4. To add fringe, cut slits at both short ends of the fabric.

5. If you like, string rolled beads (see page 14) on the fringe. Tie knots in the fringe below the beads.

Cut the material and draw some patterns. . .

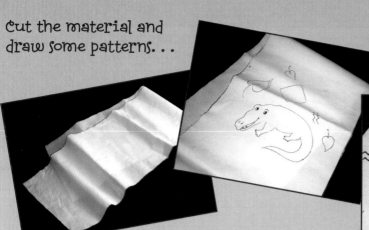

Add your own touches to make it colorful. . .

Add fringe and beads. . .

Proudly drape your African clothes over your shirt or dress on Kwanzaa!

Holiday Hint:

Many patterns woven into cloth in Africa have special meanings. Choose symbols from the patterns and explanations on pages 27–29 that say something about you or about Kwanzaa.

Strip-Quilt Mkeka

Kwanzaa symbols are placed on a mkeka (m-KAY-kah), or mat. Kente (KEN-tay) cloth from the country of Ghana is a common mkeka. The cloth is made from long, colorful strips of cotton that are sewn together.

What You Will Need:

- pencil
- ruler
- scissors
- clear contact paper
- fabric scraps, ribbon, yarn, straw, or other natural materials

1. Use a ruler to measure two 12- by 18-inch rectangles from clear contact paper. Cut out the rectangles.

2. Place one rectangle, sticky side up, on a flat surface.

3. Cut small scraps of fabric or other material into different shapes.

4. Arrange the materials on the contact paper. Try layering different materials on top of one another. Leave a ½-inch border all around the mat.

5. When your design is done, cover it with the second sheet of contact paper. The sticky side should face down this time.

6. Smooth and seal all the edges by pressing them together.

Carefully cut the material. . .

Be creative and add different objects. . .

Your finished mkeka will be unique!

Holiday Hint:

Making mats and quilts from fabric scraps is also an African-American tradition. Combine these crafts to make strip-quilt mkekas as gifts during Kwanzaa.

Words to Know

community—People with common interests living together in a particular area or location.

cooperative economics—Working together to build and maintain stores, shops, and businesses to profit as a community.

creativity—The ability to come up with or invent new things or ideas.

faith—To believe strongly in yourself, your abilities, and the community in which you live.

group work and responsibility—To build and maintain a community together.

principle—A set of values that guide people's actions in certain situations.

purpose—A goal to be achieved. The purpose during Kwanzaa is to make the community better.

respect—To give special attention or consideration.

self-determination—Having a strong will or making a decision to become a better person.

traditions—Ideas, customs, stories, or beliefs that are passed down from one generation to the next.

tribal—Relating to a social group made up of people living together in a community.

unique—One-of-a-kind, special.

unity—Being in agreement, togetherness, and harmony within a family, community, nation, or group of people.

Patterns

Use tracing paper to copy the patterns on these pages. Ask an adult to help you cut and trace the shapes onto construction paper.

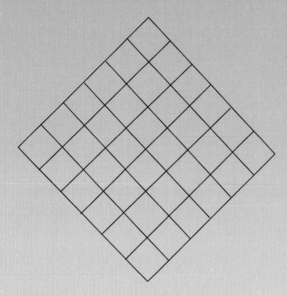

checkerboard—Earth and spirit or light and dark.

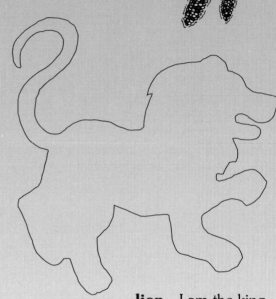

lion—I am the king.

pineapple—No pain, no gain.

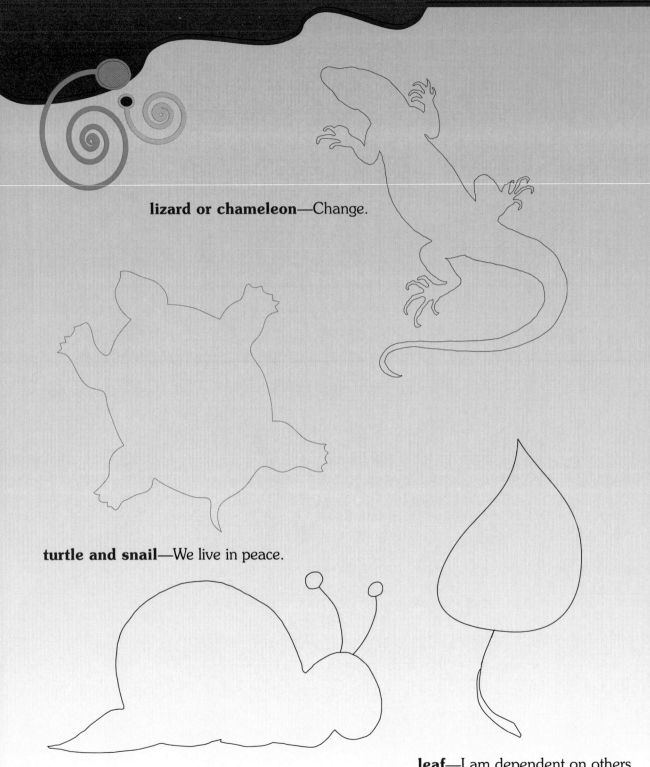

lizard or chameleon—Change.

turtle and snail—We live in peace.

leaf—I am dependent on others.

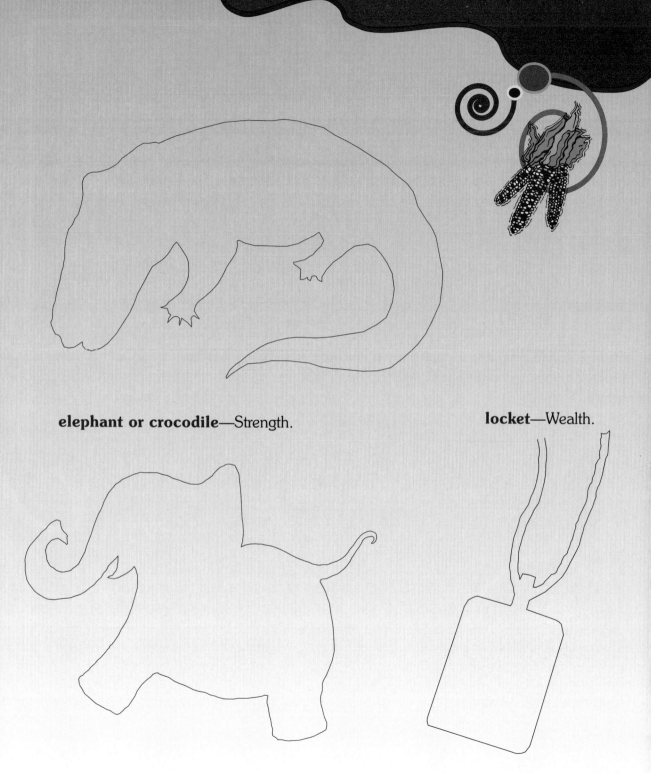

elephant or crocodile—Strength.

locket—Wealth.

Reading About Kwanzaa

Ford, Juwanda G. *Together for Kwanzaa*. New York: Random House Children's Books, 2000.

Gayle, Sharon Shavers. *Kwanzaa: An African-American Holiday*. Mahwah, N.J.: Troll Communications, LLC., 1994.

Gnojewski, Carol. *Kwanzaa: Seven Days of African-American Pride*. Berkeley Heights, N.J.: Enslow Publishers, 2004.

Medearis, Angela Shelf. *The Seven Days of Kwanzaa: How to Celebrate Them*. New York: Scholastic, Inc., 1994.

Internet Addresses

Kwanzaa Time at Kids Domain

Crafts, activities, and e-cards can be found at this fun Web site!

<http://www.kidsdomain.com/holiday/kwanzaa>

The Official Kwanzaa Web Site

This interesting and informative site offers everything you need to know about Kwanzaa.

<http://www.officialkwanzaawebsite.org>

index